Quantum Leaps
Game-Changing Strategies for Personal Development

Zachary Henry Bell

Table of Contents

1. Introduction 2
2. Understanding the Quantum Leap Approach to Personal Development 3
   - 2.1. The Philosophy Behind Quantum Leaping 3
   - 2.2. The Mechanics of a Quantum Leap 4
   - 2.3. The Potential and Promise of Quantum Leaping 4
   - 2.4. Quantum Leaping: A Journey, not a Destination 5
3. Rewiring Your Mindset: A Deep Dive into Cognitive Processes 6
   - 3.1. Understanding Cognitive Processes 6
   - 3.2. Rewiring Your Mindset 7
   - 3.3. Applying Mindset Rewiring Tools 8
   - 3.4. From Theory to Practice: A Comprehensive Exercise List 9
4. Unleashing Your Inner Potential: Tools and Techniques 11
   - 4.1. Utilizing Meditation and Mindfulness 11
   - 4.2. Embracing Neuroplasticity: Impressions to Expressions 12
   - 4.3. Broadening Perspectives: The Power of Diverse Experiences 12
   - 4.4. The Role of Physical Wellness: How Body Impacts Mind 13
5. The Role of Emotion in Quantum Leaps: From Fear to Fuel 15
   - 5.1. The Fundamental Dualism: Fear and Fuel 15
   - 5.2. Fear as a Catalyst for Change 16
   - 5.3. Transforming Fear into Fuel 16
   - 5.4. Fear as a Guide Towards Unexplored Territories 16
   - 5.5. The Empowerment of Taking Action 17
   - 5.6. Taking Flight: Fear as the Fuel 17
6. The Power of Goal Setting in Quantum Leaps 18
   - 6.1. The Science Behind Goals 18
   - 6.2. The Synergy of Quantum Thinking and Goal Setting ... 19

- 6.3. Setting Your Quantum Goals: Concrete, Yet Boundaryless ... 19
- 6.4. From Fear to Fuel: The Role of Emotion in Quantum Goal Setting ... 20
- 6.5. Implementing Quantum Goals ... 20
- 6.6. Goal Sequencing ... 21
- 6.7. Iterative Goal Refinement ... 21

7. Embracing Failure as a Tool for Rapid Development ... 22
   - 7.1. The Paradox of Failures ... 22
   - 7.2. The Multitude of Lessons Embedded in Failure ... 23
   - 7.3. Reframing Failure: From Deterrence to Fuel ... 23
   - 7.4. Building Authentic Confidence through Failure ... 24
   - 7.5. Case Studies: Harnessing The Power of Failure ... 25

8. Building Resilience: Your Cushion Against Setbacks ... 26
   - 8.1. The Definition and Importance of Resilience ... 26
   - 8.2. Building Resilience: A Deeper Examination ... 27
   - 8.3. Practical Approaches to Strengthen Resilience ... 28
   - 8.4. Transforming Setbacks into Comebacks ... 28
   - 8.5. Conclusion ... 29

9. Actualizing Quantum Leaps: Action Steps and Practical Applications ... 30
   - 9.1. The Art of Manifestation ... 30
   - 9.2. Transformative Action: The Pillar of Actualization ... 31
   - 9.3. Fear as a Jumping Point, Not a Stumbling Block ... 31
   - 9.4. Anchoring Growth: Building Success Structures ... 32

10. Sustaining Growth: Maintaining Your Quantum Leap Momentum ... 33
    - 10.1. The Dynamics of Momentum ... 33
    - 10.2. Progress Checkpoints: Measuring Growth ... 34
    - 10.3. Nurturing Self-Commitment and Discipline ... 34
    - 10.4. Adaptability: Key to Long-Term Progress ... 35

10.5. Summing it Up 35
11. Case Studies: Real-Life Applications of Quantum Leaps in Personal Development 37
    11.1. The Story of Rebecca: Unleashing Inner Potential 37
    11.2. The Transformation of Peter: Turning Failure into a Stepping Stone 38
    11.3. Jane's Journey: Building Resilience and Bouncing Back 38
    11.4. Matthew's Metamorphosis: The Quantum Leap in Embracing Change 38
    11.5. Natalie's Narrative: The Power of Effective Goal Setting ... 39

The only limit to our realization of tomorrow will be our doubts of today.

— Franklin D. Roosevelt

Chapter 1. Introduction

Special Report: Quantum Leaps: Game-Changing Strategies for Personal Development

Unleash the boundless capacity within you as we plunge into the remarkable world of personal development. Welcome to our Special Report, "Quantum Leaps: Game-Changing Strategies for Personal Development." This groundbreaking guide amplifies your understanding of personal growth, emphasizing the value of quantum thinking. We illuminate the path to your highest potential by fusing profound insights with actionable strategies—enabling genuine, substantial growth that will pervade every aspect of your life. This isn't about the typical, measured steps of traditional self-help guidance. This is about profound, transformative changes that can catapult you towards your goals like never before. Intuitive, exhilarating, and fundamentally empowering, this report is your ticket to an extraordinary journey of self-discovery and transcendent growth. Seize this moment, take the quantum leap, and be prepared for a metamorphosis beyond imagination!

Chapter 2. Understanding the Quantum Leap Approach to Personal Development

Before diving headfirst into this vast realm, it is prudent to define clearly what we mean by a "quantum leap." In physics, a quantum leap can be defined as an abrupt transition, often involving considerable energy, between two states. In the context of personal development, a quantum leap refers to a significant, sudden progress towards one's potential or goals—propelling you far beyond the previously perceived limits of what was thought possible. This metaphorical leap transcends the realm of moderate improvements and incremental moves of traditional personal growth strategy. It is about making massive strides, not modest steps.

2.1. The Philosophy Behind Quantum Leaping

To better understand this, we must first explore the philosophy that underpins quantum leaping. It is based on a growth mindset—a fundamental belief in the ability to change, learn, and improve over time. This mindset roots acceptance in the fact that limitations are often self-imposed and can be transcended with the right tools and attitude. Those embracing the quantum leap approach perceive every challenge as an opportunity to grow, holding onto the universal truth that human beings possess vast untapped potential. They discard the old linear way of thinking, instead focusing on exponential growth, where the benefits massively outweigh the efforts put in.

Quantum leaps also invoke the principles of reframing and paradigm shifting, key concepts in many psychological and coaching techniques. It encourages the liberation of one's mind from the constraints of past experiences, creating new spaces and possibilities for transformative growth.

2.2. The Mechanics of a Quantum Leap

To truly comprehend the quantum leap in personal development, a good association to draw upon is the lotus flower. Birthed in the dirty and dark mud, the lotus must go through a transformational event—the breaking of its seed and the extending of its roots, before it can rise above and blossom into a beautiful flower. Much like the lotus flower, a quantum leap in personal development is a transformative event that changes the events, milestones, and narrative of the individual.

The mechanics of this leap are centered around the process of 'letting go.' This could be letting go of fears, insecurities, limiting beliefs, or debilitating habits. It highlights the importance of moving past comfortable yet restrictive practices, to truly experience remarkable growth.

While a quantum leap suggests a sudden, large jump, it is essential to recognize that it is not abrupt. Instead, it is a consciously initiated and thoughtfully executed process composed of numerous 'micro-leaps.' These are subsequently expressed as one big leap in personal development. Every decision, every moment of courage, every reframed belief, contributes to this transformative jump.

2.3. The Potential and Promise of Quantum Leaping

Although quantum leaps require courage and tenacity, the rewards it promises are unparalleled. It leads to transformative growth, rather than restrained, incremental improvements. It allows individuals to bypass years of gradual progress, overcoming substantial hurdles or making marked improvements in a relatively short space of time.

In essence, by embracing the quantum leap approach, you open yourself to an extraordinary level of development, journeying beyond the ordinary and stepping into the extraordinary. You accelerate your growth trajectory, expanding your capabilities exponentially, thereby maximizing your full potential.

2.4. Quantum Leaping: A Journey, not a Destination

The strategy of quantum leaps is not just about the leap itself; it's about the courage to leap, the exhilaration of leaping, and the transformation that happens within and throughout this process. It's a powerful journey of self-discovery and self-realization – a journey that reveals who we truly are and what we are truly capable of.

This chapter has only opened the door to the world of quantum leaping, signaling that going beyond the comfort zone, reframing thoughts, and executing action are the fulcrums on which quantum personal development pivots. As we delve further into the subsequent chapters, we flesh out the mechanics, strategies, and applications of these concepts, grounding this unique approach in practical, actionable insights that promise to catalyze your personal development in unparalleled, extraordinary ways.

Chapter 3. Rewiring Your Mindset: A Deep Dive into Cognitive Processes

In the journey of self-development and personal expansion, understanding the intricacies of our cognition—how we perceive, process, and react to the world around us—provides an invaluable foundation. Adopting an innovative, transformative approach to mindset shift can illuminate a pathway towards new perspectives, unprecedented insights, and a profound evolution in personal growth.

3.1. Understanding Cognitive Processes

The human cognitive process comprises five core components: perception, attention, memory, language, and executive functions. Each plays a pivotal role in shaping our thoughts, beliefs, and ultimately, our realities. By rewiring our conceptual grid, we can foster an environment ripe for quantum leaps in personal development.

Perception is the gathering of information through our five senses. It's our initial contact with our surroundings and underscores how we interpret our environment. Through understanding perception, we gain insight into how we frame our reality based on what we perceive. Altering this initial framing can lead to drastic shifts in understanding and perspective.

Attention, on the other hand, involves the active manipulation of our cognitive processes as we focus on specific elements in our environment. With an average attention span dwindling due to an increasingly frenetic digital environment, training our brains to cultivate attention and focus can unlock immense mental capacities.

Thirdly, *memory*—our mind's ability to encode, store, and retrieve information—is a valuable reservoir of wisdom and experience. Enhancing the fluidity with which we can tap into this wellspring fosters a more holistic, informed worldview.

Language, our tool for encoding and decoding meaning, helps us communicate and comprehend our inner and outer world. Reframing our linguistic understanding can drastically transform our personal narratives, propelling us towards profound self-discovery.

Lastly, our *executive functions* encompass a series of higher mental capacities, such as reasoning, problem-solving, and decision making. Gaining mastery over these allows us to navigate our lives with purpose, intention, and clarity.

3.2. Rewiring Your Mindset

Renewing the mind begins with understanding these cognitive processes, but the journey of rewiring isn't solely analytical. It's about shifting paradigms, adopting empowering beliefs, and nurturing an environment for transformative thought to foster. Below are some strategies for rewiring the mind for quantum personal development.

1. *Mindfulness and Meditation*: Routine mindfulness practice and meditation are potent tools for cognitive restructuring. They help you observe your thought patterns without judgment, allowing you to consciously select the ones that serve your growth. Moreover, meditation improves focus, memory, and emotional control, making it an invaluable addition to your personal development regimen.

2. *Cognitive Restructuring*: Often used in cognitive-behavioral

therapy, cognitive restructuring involves identifying and challenging irrational or maladaptive thoughts. It's about understanding the difference between objective reality and our subjective interpretations of it. With practice, cognitive restructuring can help us develop healthier, more accurate cognitions.

3. *Affirmations*: Positive affirmations are statements that help you challenge and overcome negative thoughts. When you repeat them often and believe in them, you can instigate positive changes in your life.

4. *Neuroplasticity Workouts*: Neuroplasticity refers to the brain's capacity to reorganize itself throughout life by forming new neural connections. Engaging our minds in new, challenging experiences stimulates this process, forging new thought paths that replace disempowering beliefs.

5. *Mindset Shift Techniques*: Various techniques like visualization, journaling, and reframing can help in making the mindset shift. Incorporating these tools into your daily routine can lead to transformative cognitive changes.

3.3. Applying Mindset Rewiring Tools

How do you apply the aforementioned tools? Begin by cultivating a heightened mindfulness practice. Next, engage in cognitive restructuring processes to pinpoint problematic thought patterns and replace them with more adaptive ones. Utilize affirmations to foster positive thinking, and challenge your brain with neuroplasticity workouts by engaging in new, stimulating activities. Finally, adopt mindset shift techniques tailored to your specific needs and goals.

Remember, the goal is not an overnight metamorphosis but rather a continuous journey of introspection, growth, and steadfast progress.

With commitment and resilience, mind rewiring can catalyze quantum leaps in your personal development journey, reshaping how you perceive yourself, others, and the world around you. A crucial element of the process rests in taking action, walking the walk in the face of all hurdles, and persistently putting these insights into practice on your journey of personal evolution.

3.4. From Theory to Practice: A Comprehensive Exercise List

To bring theory into practice, here are some exercises that you can add to your everyday routine to rewire your mindset:

[i] Mindfulness and Meditation: Start with 5 to 10 minutes of mindfulness meditation daily, slowly increasing the time as you grow more comfortable.

[ii] Cognitive Restructuring: Keep a thought diary. When you experience negative emotions, detail what happened, your thoughts during the instance, and evidence for and against that thought. Then, find an alternative, objective thought.

[iii] Affirmations: Write a list of positive affirmations tailored to your specific goals and needs. Repeat them aloud to yourself every morning and evening.

[iv] Neuroplasticity Workouts: Engage in brain-boosting activities like reading, puzzles, learning a new language, or playing a musical instrument.

[v] Mindset Shift Techniques: Use visualization techniques to imagine your desired outcomes. Journal about your feelings, challenges, and progress.

The journey to rewiring your mindset and subsequent personal development takes both time and patience. By breaking your ultimate goals into manageable, daily tasks, you can foster tangible growth that will gradually accumulate into sweeping transformations. Merely remember, progress, not perfection, is the key. Continue the journey with passion and persistence, as the power to achieve quantum leaps in personal growth lies within your mind.

Chapter 4. Unleashing Your Inner Potential: Tools and Techniques

Diving headfirst into the world of personal development invites us to grapple with our innate potential—our tremendous capacity, lying dormant, vitually untapped, waiting to be ignited. Understanding the ways in which we can catalyze this potential is critical, involving an exploration of tools, techniques, and methodologies that propel us beyond the bounds of our typical modes of thought and action. These methods drive us into the realm of the extraordinary, enabling us to tap into our deepest reservoirs of creativity, productivity, and progression.

4.1. Utilizing Meditation and Mindfulness

Our journey begins with perhaps the most profound inner technology at our disposal—meditation and mindfulness. Initially, mindfulness may seem deceptively simple, merely involves staying present to our experiences moment by moment. Yet, the actual practice and its reverberating impact throughout our life is far more profound.

Delving deeper, you recognize mindfulness as an incredible avenue for quieting the ceaseless chatter of our minds. It allows us to tap into an inner tranquillity and clarity that tunes us into the symphony of the present moment. Meditation, on the other hand, sharpens our focus, greases the wheels of cognition, and diffuses inherent stress and anxieties. The ripple effects of these practices are substantial, priming the mind to take quantum leaps in personal development.

By cultivating a regular meditation and mindfulness practice, we foster mental bandwidth, sharpen concentration, and enhance receptivity to new experiences. While mindfulness roots us to the impermanent nature of our thoughts and sensations, meditation paves the way for blurring the confines of the mind and tapping into unexplored reservoirs of potentiality.

4.2. Embracing Neuroplasticity: Impressions to Expressions

Neuroplasticity is the cornerstone of unleashing our potential. Our brain's extraordinary ability to form, reform, and reshape its intricate network of neural connections is a testament to human evolution. These connections, sculpted by our experiences and thought patterns, are not just reactive but proactive—our cognitive abilities are not set in stone but as malleable as clay.

Residing at the heart of neuroplasticity is the recognition that our minds can change our brains, and consequently our lives. Capitalizing on this astonishing fact dramatically upscales our personal development. To harness neuroplasticity, intentionally cultivating positive mental states can gradually transform these fleeting states into enduring neural traits. Over time, neuroplasticity allows dramatic transformations, reshaping our mindsets, attitudes, and reactions.

4.3. Broadening Perspectives: The Power of Diverse Experiences

Our perspectives shape our reality. Yet, the strength of our perspectives lies in their diversity. Experimenting with novel experiences, challenging our ingrained notions, meeting people from different walks of life, or simply shaking up our routines, can endow us with fresh perspectives. This explosion of novelty jolts our minds, provoking reflections, stirring creativity, and stimulating breakthroughs.

Often, we tend to stay anchored in our comfortable bubbles, looping our established routines incessantly. However, stepping into the unfamiliar broadens our understanding, imparts resilience, and enriches our experiences. Embracing this can be transformational, driving a wave of exponential personal development. The novel enrichment of our cognitive schemata opens us up to unforeseen possibilities, thereby shattering conventional limitations.

4.4. The Role of Physical Wellness: How Body Impacts Mind

Lastly, our capabilities, mental and emotional stamina hinge heavily on our physical vitality. Food, exercise, sleep—all these factors influence our cognitive function, mood, and overall well-being. When we compromise on these, we inadvertently dampen our potential.

A nourishing diet fuels our cognitive machinery. Regular exercise, meanwhile, elevates our mood, sharpens memory, boosts creativity, and acts as a powerful antidote to stress, anxiety, and depression. Consistent sleep rejuvenates our mind-body system, infusing us with renewed vigor to engage productively with the world.

Implementing a healthy lifestyle is an integral part of the road-map to unleash inner potential. It's a window to connecting with our sensation-rich, embodied existence while also forming a sturdy pillar for personal development.

By deploying these tools and techniques conscientiously, we engineer a conducive environment for the mind to tango with potentiality. The bridling energy, the fervid curiosity, the razor-sharp focus—these are the embers of a mind aflame with the strength that comes from within, now brought to utter fruition. Engage with this, cultivate it, and watch as your inner potential unfurls like the most magnificent of flowers, radiant and bountiful. Let this journey of self-discovery push you beyond the imaginable, launching you into spaces of unprecedented personal development, reaching for the stars and grabbing them with both hands.

Chapter 5. The Role of Emotion in Quantum Leaps: From Fear to Fuel

The human emotional landscape has long been a subject of passionate investigation, and one of its most important aspects is the interplay between fear and fuel. At this juncture where fear can morph into motivation, a quantum leap in personal development becomes plausible. But what is this chemistry, how does it work in the backdrop of our psyche, and how can we turn our fears into the very fuel that propels our inner growth rocket into the stratosphere of self-actualization? To answer these and delve tangibly into nuances, let's embark on a meticulous expedition.

5.1. The Fundamental Dualism: Fear and Fuel

Fear and motivation are flip sides of the same metaphysical coin. Fear, an ancient evolutionary mechanism, generated by the amygdala, resides at the very core of our emotions, designed to protect us from danger, and has secured our survival as a species for eons. Fuel, on the other hand, is the impetus for growth, a psychological driving force rooted in our insatiable striving for achievement and self-realization.

A dualistic relationship exists between these two elements, where the transition from fear to fuel can be seen as a process that involves recognizing fear as an invitation to step out of our comfort zone, then transforming it into positive energy to achieve our personal developmental goals.

5.2. Fear as a Catalyst for Change

Fear initially manifests as an adversity or obstacle in our path of personal growth. However, when scrutinized, it might just be the catalyst we need to spark growth. Fear can spur us to action by illuminating the gaps in our knowledge or skills, providing a tangible, if tension-fraught, frame of reference against which we can measure and plan our progress.

To leverage this perspective, we need to acknowledge fear for what it is: an evolutionary response to perceived danger or inadequacy, a primal nudge to prepare us either physically or psychologically for the upcoming challenge.

5.3. Transforming Fear into Fuel

Transformation of fear into fuel begins with the mental reframing of fear as an empowering guide towards areas of life needing critical attention and improvement. By strategically embracing fear, we can funnel it into motivation for change. The primary steps involve acknowledging the fear, understanding its root cause, and thereafter, devising a calculated, systematic approach towards confronting it—a strategic deviation from the instinctual fear response.

Understanding your fear and its origins marks the beginning of transformation. Practice compassionate inquiry into your fear, asking yourself questions about its roots, its triggers, and its patterns. Oftentimes, our fears are relics from past experiences, which have imprinted a deep unequivocal message: avoid at all cost.

5.4. Fear as a Guide Towards Unexplored Territories

By acknowledging these fears, we can start treating them as signposts leading towards unexplored territories in our personal development. They flag up opportunities for personal growth, as the area causing fear is often an area where we lack experience, knowledge, or confidence. By confronting the fear, we push the boundaries of our comfort zones, launching ourselves into a new realm of personal growth.

5.5. The Empowerment of Taking Action

In the metamorphosis from fear to fuel, action can be seen as the chrysalis stage. Taking robust action in the face of fear dispels the phantom image fear so often draws up. The instances of facing fears topple the domino effect by providing positive reinforcement that, yes, you can navigate the terrain of your fear.

5.6. Taking Flight: Fear as the Fuel

In the physical world, transformation of potential energy into kinetic energy propels forward motion. Interestingly, the same analogy applies to our internal world. As we've learned to manage and transform fear—an energy source formerly holding us back—it becomes the fuel that catapults us into the realm of manifesting our full potential.

In conclusion, deciphering the intricate relationship between fear and fuel forms a pivotal piece of the quantum leaps puzzle. Realizing fear as a potential motivator, fear as a guide, and fear as fuel, we can reconceptualize our fear-based impediments into powerful propellers on the winds of personal growth—an essential quantum leap from fear to achieving unimagined portraits of possibility and personal development. Embrace the fear, harness the fear, and let it charge your sails towards the horizon of your highest potential.

Chapter 6. The Power of Goal Setting in Quantum Leaps

Just like the pivotal chirp of a quantum bit that sends powerful signals ripping through circuits, introducing an irreversible, instantaneous change, goals serve as critical catalysts in our journey of personal development. They are the destinations on our personal roadmap, the stars that guide us, and the striking steps towards quantum leaps. In this landscape of personal transformation, it is paramount to understand the intricacies of goal setting in the context of quantum leaps.

6.1. The Science Behind Goals

The human brain is an incredible organic computer, capable of handling vast amounts of data, forming intricate connections, and driving motivation. However, it often lacks direction without goals, merely processing life without clear intent or purpose. Goals serve as the compass for your mental energies, fostering focus and channeling your cognitive capabilities towards desired outcomes. The potent ability of well-set goals to stimulate neuronal activation and guide our behavior has been well-documented in numerous psychology and neuroscience studies, emphasizing that setting goals is far from a vague, abstract idea—it's a science.

A goal generates a certain threshold of tension in the mind, a cognitive discrepancy between our current state and the aspirational one. This tension creates an inherent drive within us to reduce the gap, setting the stage for effort, persistence, and concentrated attention—all critical ingredients for a quantum leap.

6.2. The Synergy of Quantum Thinking and Goal Setting

Quantum thinking, unlike classical thinking, embraces ambiguity, uncertainty, and the infinite potential of possibilities. When fused with the pragmatic, focused process of goal setting, it triggers an extraordinary synergy. This integration of quantum thinking lifts goal setting from mere incremental progression towards a transformative leap, serving to propel a shift from linear progression to exponential development.

Your goals, when informed by quantum thinking, become fluid and limitless. They are able to exist in several states at once, can move between states in an instant, and most excitingly, their potential can be exponentially more than the sum of its parts, reflecting the principles of quantum entanglement.

6.3. Setting Your Quantum Goals: Concrete, Yet Boundaryless

While it might seem paradoxical, quantum goals are both concrete and boundaryless. Consider your goals as coordinates in the vast landscape of possibility. You need precise data points to navigate, yet there is no border to the expanse you can explore. In setting these goals, strive for specificity and clarity. Define what you want in a measurable, observable way. This specificity not only serves as a clear point of focus but also releases potent motivational energy to propel the journey.

However, avoid becoming so fixated on the specified goals that you restrict your potential. Quantum leaps, by definition, are leaps into the unknown or unanticipated, therefore permit yourself the freedom to revise, adapt and even overhaul goals as necessary. When setting goals, maintain a delicate balance between the concrete and the far-reaching, between the specific and the limitless.

6.4. From Fear to Fuel: The Role of Emotion in Quantum Goal Setting

Emotions play a critical role in the realm of quantum goal setting. Often, fear—the fear of what might happen if you fail or even if you succeed—can paralyze our efforts. However, emotions like fear can be harnessed as potent fuel for your quantum leap, reframed into a challenge to overcome, or an obstacle that opens the door to growth once conquered.

The process of setting such ambitious goals can also be intrinsically inspiring. The very idea of what you could achieve may serve to ignite a passion and unearth a fervor for growth you never knew existed within you. Embrace these emotions, and allow them to motivate and guide you as you traverse the uncertain, thrilling landscape of quantum leaps.

6.5. Implementing Quantum Goals

The heart of quantum goal setting rests in its actual implementation. Channel the principles of quantum thinking—creativity, flexibility, intuition, and boundless potential—into the process of designing your actionable steps towards these goals. Remember, quantum leaps do not merely imply thinking big, but thinking differently.

Following the setting of your quantum goals, establish an action plan brimming with novel approaches, daring decisions, and shifts in perspective that would make it feasible to realize these goals. The key lies in maintaining a resilient determination while embracing change and welcoming unforeseen pathways.

6.6. Goal Sequencing

Just as in quantum computing, where effective sequencing can unlock an exponential increase in computational power, effective sequencing of tasks related to your goals can yield heightened efficiency and progress. Leveraging the principle of 'superposition', attempt to identify tasks that can be done in parallel without diluting your focus or overwhelming you. Learning to prioritize effectively can help direct your efforts where they are most needed, accelerating your progress towards your quantum goals.

6.7. Iterative Goal Refinement

Our understanding and desires continually evolve as we develop and learn through our experiences. Consequently, so should our goals. Going back and reevaluating your goals from time to time is a necessary part of the process. This process of iterative refinement ensures that your quantum goals continue to align with your evolving aspirations and abilities.

The power of goal setting in the context of quantum leaps is immense, marrying the limitless potential of quantum thinking with the concrete motivation of well-formulated ambitions. As you venture into this intricate, thrilling voyage of personal development, remember the value of effective goal setting, and harness its potential as the wind in your sails for your quantum leap journey.

Chapter 7. Embracing Failure as a Tool for Rapid Development

Failure is an inevitable part of life—a brutal, yet integral force that shapes us, refines us, and despite the discomfort it brings, empowers us. As counter-intuitive as it may sound, embracing failure can become an incredibly powerful tool for rapid personal development. While our fears and societal conditioning often guide us to avoid failure at all costs, we will reveal in this chapter why this perception needs to be reframed.

7.1. The Paradox of Failures

From the moment we set foot in this world, widespread narratives regarding success and failure frame our understanding of them as polar opposites. Success is celebrated, desired, and sought after, while failure is berated, dreaded, and avoided. This dominant interpretation of failure often results in an adversarial relationship, an approach we need to revise.

It is essential to acknowledge that failure, in its true essence, is not an adversary, but rather a guide. It exposes our weaknesses, opens our eyes to our mistakes, and prompts a reassessment of our strategies. Embracing failure ultimately paves the way for a nuanced understanding of our journeys, facilitating insight and growth at an unprecedented pace.

7.2. The Multitude of Lessons Embedded in Failure

Every failure, as crushing as it may feel, holds within it a multitude of lessons. It is through conscious introspection, open-hearted acceptance, and a shift in perspective that we can access these hidden treasures.

One important lesson failure teaches us is humility. It reminds us of our human fallibility, severs our ties with excessive pride, and prompts us to be gracious even in our shortcomings. Humility engenders an openness to learning, to acknowledge our errors and develop strategies to circumvent them in the future.

Another lesson, intrinsically tied to embracing failure, is resilience. The very act of rising from the ashes of failure, dusting ourselves off, and stepping into the arena once again speaks volumes about our intrinsic capacity to recover and progress.

Finally, failure presents the invaluable lesson of persistence. If we study the lives of those who have achieved extraordinary feats, a common thread weaves their stories together—the tenacity to persist in the face of relentless failures. It is evidence that when we persist, despite our failures, we significantly enhance our chances of eventual success.

7.3. Reframing Failure: From Deterrence to Fuel

The process of reframing our understanding and relationship with failure is both challenging and invigorating. It demands a complete paradigm shift—from viewing failure as a deterrent to considering it as a refuelling station that supplies invaluable insights, learning opportunities, and pockets of growth.

This reframing can be effectively achieved through the following steps:

1. Identifying Our Fear: Our first step is to discern the base fear that fuels our aversion towards failure. Is it the fear of judgment and social ridicule? The fear of self-doubt and a bruised ego? Once we've identified this fear, we can begin to work on designing strategies to overcome it.
2. Acceptance: The next step is acceptance. We need to accept that failure is embedded in the fabric of success. Acceptance here is not mere resignation or surrender, but a bold step forward to confront, understand, and engage with the entire process of failure openly.
3. Reframing: Once we've identified our fear and accepted the underlying reality of failure, it's time to reframe our view. We must choose a perspective that doesn't perceive failure as a dead-end, but as a detour to an alternative route—one that may offer a faster or more enriching journey to our goals.

7.4. Building Authentic Confidence through Failure

Another transformative benefit of embracing failure is the construction of authentic and unshakeable confidence. Society often misrepresents confidence as the absence of failure. In reality, true confidence is built on the firm foundation of acknowledged, understood, and surmounted failures. Moreover, reveling in the lessons and growth opportunities arising from failure erodes the fear of future failures, and in this, we find our strength and genuine confidence.

7.5. Case Studies: Harnessing The Power of Failure

In the annals of history and the stories of contemporary success, case studies abound where failure served not as the end of the road, but as a turning point — an essential catalyst for personal growth and eventual triumph.

Thomas Edison, the renowned inventor, famously said, "I have not failed. I've just found 10,000 ways that won't work." Edison's revolutionary perspective of seeing each failure as a valuable lesson in what not to do eventually led to his creation of the successful working light bulb—an invention that drastically changed the course of human history.

In another instance, Steve Jobs, the co-founder of Apple Inc., after being ousted from his own company, considered this failure as a liberating experience. He reflected, learnt, ventured into other businesses, and fine-tuned his strategies—actions which lay the groundwork for his smashing comeback to Apple years later.

In both cases, embracing their failures, gleaning lessons from them, and then using these experiences as stepping stones played a pivotal role in their exceptional success stories.

Exchange the conventional narrative of failure with an empowering one: Failures are, in fact, the stepping stones to success, which, once embraced, accelerates personal development. Rising from our failures and launching ourselves once again into the pursuit of our dreams, we learn to build resilience, embrace humility, persist steadfastly, and develop authentic confidence. This is the power of reframing failure—turning it from an insurmountable obstacle into a tool for rapid and transformative personal development.

Chapter 8. Building Resilience: Your Cushion Against Setbacks

Resilience: it's a term often bandied about in personal development literature and psychology studies alike. Its potency as a trait cannot be overstated—indeed, it forms the bedrock of our capacity to cope with life's inevitable challenges. So, what does it mean to be resilient, and how can we foster this valuable attribute? Let's explore this concept in intricate detail.

8.1. The Definition and Importance of Resilience

By simple definition, resilience refers to our ability to bounce back from adversity. It is our biological elasticity that enables us to recover from losses, traumas, stress, disappointments, and failures. From a quantum leap perspective, resilience brings a paradigm shift, an opportunity to transcend mere survival and promote thriving in the face of adversities.

The importance of resilience to personal development is paramount. Consider it as your secret weapon, your fortress of mental and emotional strength that protects against setbacks. Without resilience, each setback would be an ending, a full stop halting our progression towards our goals. With resilience, however, setbacks transform into stepping stones, fostering growth, learning, and progress.

8.2. Building Resilience: A Deeper Examination

Now that we've established the critical role of resilience, the question arises - How does one nurture this capacity?

The first step is to understand that building resilience is not a singular act, but a continual process, a lifestyle. It's not merely about recovering quickly but also growing stronger and wiser from each experience.

Framework for Enhancing Resilience

1. **Emotional Awareness**: Cultivate the skill of recognizing and articulating your feelings. Emotional awareness helps you navigate your feelings effectively, instead of being blind-sided by them during a crisis.
2. **Positive Outlook**: Foster a positive mindset. Though it is natural to focus on problems during hardship, we must concentrate on possibilities and solutions.
3. **Support Systems**: Building and maintaining strong relationships play a crucial role. Resilience doesn't mean handling problems alone; a robust support backbone empowers us to withstand challenges more effectively.
4. **Accepting Change**: Embrace change as inevitable, and adapt accordingly. This adaptability equips us to navigate unexpected crises and loss.
5. **Goal-Oriented**: Maintain focus on your goals. They act as the North Star, guiding you through dark and difficult times.
6. **Self-Care**: Prioritize physical health and psychological well-being. A healthy body and mind augment coping mechanisms during adversities.

8.3. Practical Approaches to Strengthen Resilience

Building resilience is an abstract concept, but it can be distilled into concrete actions. Here are the practical strategies to bolster resilience:

Steps for Strengthening Resilience
1. **Mindfulness Practice**: Mindfulness helps anchor us to the present moment, enhancing our ability to cope with current challenges, rather than worrying unduly about the past or future.
2. **Reframing Thoughts**: Transform negative thought patterns into positive ones. It's about taking charge of your cognitive processes, shaping them to work for you, not against you.
3. **Cultivating Gratitude**: Focus on the positive things in your life, no matter how trivial. This approach nurtures positivity, helping you to get through difficult situations.
4. **Seeking Support**: Don't hesitate to lean on your support system when faced with challenges. Remember, admitting you need help is an indicator of strength, not weakness.
5. **Healthy Lifestyle**: Engage in regular physical activity, eat a balanced diet, ensure adequate sleep, and avoid harmful substances. They strengthen your body, mind, and in turn, your resilience.

8.4. Transforming Setbacks into Comebacks

Once you've begun building your resilience, it's time to apply this potent trait to specific problems. Each setback, each stumbling block, lets you put your resilience into practice and emerge stronger from the experience.

Remember, setbacks are not only inevitable but also indispensable for growth. They are a part of your unique journey toward self-development. By deploying resilience, you not only ensure quick recovery but also transform these setbacks into comebacks, emerging stronger, wiser, and more capable.

8.5. Conclusion

Cultivating resilience can sound like an ominous task, but whenever you confront and make it through adversity, you are actively building your resilience. The process of building resilience is ongoing and becomes a part of who you are, not something you turn on in the face of adversity. By applying these steps to your daily life, you can increase your ability to bounce back from setbacks, thereby aiding your quantum leap journey towards personal development.

Take the journey one step at a time, remain patient, and soon you may find yourself more capable and resilient than ever before. Embrace the obstacle; your time to shine is right on the other side of the challenge!

Chapter 9. Actualizing Quantum Leaps: Action Steps and Practical Applications

As we plunge into the compelling realm of actualizing quantum leaps, let's remember this crucial principle: knowledge without application is simply a decorated ignorance. After furnishing your mind with the powerful insights about quantum leaps in personal development, it's time to ground this understanding, translate it into practice, and reap its extraordinary benefits. The focus of this chapter is to provide concrete, actionable steps and pragmatic applications. We'll guide you through the process, arming you with empowering tools to transform knowledge into actions that yield tangible results.

9.1. The Art of Manifestation

Understanding manifestation—one of the definitive factors for actualizing quantum leaps—is like unveiling the miraculous alchemy that transforms thoughts into reality. It's the act of turning inward, harnessing your intrinsic power, and directing it outwards to mold the reality you desire and deserve. To stand on the threshold of your quantum leap, you must align your actions, thoughts, and emotions, channelling them towards your desired state with unwavering commitment and crystalline clarity.

1. *Visualization:* This technique involves representing your goals in your mind's eye. Paint a detailed picture encompassing all five senses. What does your goal look like? What does achieving it feel like? The more details your mind grasps, the more it's motivated to act towards it.

2. *Affirmations:* Frame positive, powerful statements that represent

your desired outcome. Affirmations program your subconscious mind, priming it for success.

3. *Action Steps:* Lastly, compile a list of actions that lead towards your goal. Following these steps diligently will embody the change you seek, translating your purpose into a reality.

9.2. Transformative Action: The Pillar of Actualization

Action—the raw, tangible, and manifesting aspect of any personal development plan—is where the rubber meets the road. The difference between stagnation and a quantum leap often rests upon an individual's willingness to take inspired, intentional actions. Here are invaluable strategies to gear you up for these transformative action steps:

1. *Break It Down:* Quantum leaps may be massive, but the action steps shouldn't intimidate you. Break your large goals into manageable chunks. This eases the overwhelming perception and fosters momentum as you tackle each smaller task progressively.
2. *Take Consistent Actions:* Progress stems from regular, consistent actions, however small. Embrace the philosophy of 'constant and never-ending improvement' and make incremental progress your daily mantra.
3. *Prioritize:* Not all actions hold equal significance. Prioritize by identifying and focusing on high-impact tasks.

9.3. Fear as a Jumping Point, Not a Stumbling Block

Fear—the eternal nemesis of human ambitions—often stands as the colossal barrier on the road to quantum leaps. Rather than surrendering to fear, use it as a pivot to propel yourself forward. Acknowledge it as an indicator of growth, a sign that you're venturing into uncharted territories and breaking free from your comfort zone. Do not dread fear; reframe it as the doorway to your growth.

9.4. Anchoring Growth: Building Success Structures

To anchor your newfound growth and keep the momentum alive, build sturdy success structures. These frameworks constitute habits, routines, and systems that support and sustain your quantum leap. Be it a morning routine that sets the tone for the day, a meditation practice that wipes the mental clutter, or a health regimen that bolsters your energy—these structures will underpin your journey towards self-actualization, keeping you grounded and focused.

To summarize, actualizing a quantum leap involves a harmonious blend of the right mindset, massive action, fear handling, and supportive success structures. Remember, the most substantial part of a quantum leap isn't merely the end result, but the transformative journey—the deep inner shifts, the shedding of old limitations, and the thrilling discovery of new territories within you. Embrace this profound journey and prepare to unlock the promised domain of growth and freedom. You can and will actualize your aspirations. Seize this extraordinary momentum and leap into your boundless potential.

Chapter 10. Sustaining Growth: Maintaining Your Quantum Leap Momentum

Following that remarkable quantum leap—your transformative journey of substantial personal growth, you now find yourself on the cusp of a new paradigm. Accustomed to the new, more evolved version of yourself, the question now is, how do you maintain this momentum? This chapter delves deeply into the strategies for sustaining the progress achieved through the Quantum Leap.

10.1. The Dynamics of Momentum

In any aspect of life, sustaining momentum can be as challenging as initiating it. Understanding the dynamics of momentum is crucial to keep moving forward with the same vigor and enthusiasm after a quantum leap.

Momentum can be likened to a heavy flywheel. It requires a considerable amount of force to get it spinning, but once it's in motion, it continues to spin, fed by its own inertia. In personal development, this inertia is the manifestation of habitual patterns that come from continuous practice, consistency, and perseverance.

It becomes crucial, then, to cultivate habits and mindsets that support your quantum leap's lodestar direction and to eliminate those that are counter-productive. The former lend strength to your inertia, helping maintain your momentum, while the latter cause friction, slowing your progress. In the process of sustaining growth, we must avoid the friction of negative habits and feed the inertia with positive practices.

10.2. Progress Checkpoints: Measuring Growth

We all know the phrase "what gets measured, gets managed." Regular assessments of your progress serve as checkpoints on your path to personal development. They gauge the effectiveness of your strategies, helping refine them for the future.

Logically placed progress checkpoints can be beneficial in providing the necessary motivation to continue. They also provide real-time feedback on your progress that can be instrumental in fine-tuning your strategies.

Progress checkpoints can be split into the following categories:

1. Quantitative Measures: These are numerically measurable parameters. They might include reading a certain number of books in a month, achieving a particular weight loss goal, or reaching a specific savings target.
2. Qualitative Measures: These are subjective assessments of personal experiences and feelings. They might involve journaling emotions, noting changes in thinking patterns, or practicing mindful awareness of your actions and responses.

Keeping track of both these measures provides a balanced perspective of your progress post the quantum leap and helps in maintaining the momentum.

10.3. Nurturing Self-Commitment and Discipline

Sustaining the growth momentum requires an unwavering commitment to continuous self-improvement and discipline to put in the effort it entails. Without self-commitment, efforts can wane and progress can buckle under the weight of complacency. Discipline, on the other hand, ensures that you follow your personal development regime diligently, even when the initial euphoria of the quantum leap has faded.

Here are some strategies to nurture self-commitment and discipline:

1. Set clear, achievable goals: Clear goals provide direction, making it easier to stay committed.
2. Stay consistent: Aim for small, consistent steps that form a much larger journey.
3. Make it a part of your routine: Whether it's reading, meditating, or any other activity, make it a daily ritual.
4. Hold yourself accountable: Be responsible for your actions, and, if possible, share your journey with someone close who can provide support and encouragement.

10.4. Adaptability: Key to Long-Term Progress

In life, change is the only constant. To maintain momentum in the ever-changing landscape of our lives, it becomes integral to remain flexible and adaptive. As we grow and evolve, the strategies that worked before may not be as effective. You must be willing to reassess, adapt, and realign your growth strategies periodically. Here, adaptability is directly proportional to long-term progress.

10.5. Summing it Up

Sustaining the growth momentum after a quantum leap is about feeding the inertia with beneficial practices, measuring progress, nurturing self-commitment, discipline, and being adaptable. While the journey may be fraught with challenges and tough times, an iron resolve towards the end goal and the willingness to keep evolving shall prove instrumental in maintaining momentum. Always remember, a quantum leap is significant, but the true victory lies in maximizing the utility of this leap and persistently marching towards greater personal development.

Chapter 11. Case Studies: Real-Life Applications of Quantum Leaps in Personal Development

Diving directly into the matter at hand, we will initiate by comprehending the significance of case studies when dissecting the real-life applications of quantum leaps in personal development. Case studies serve as valuable tools for studying this innovative approach towards personal growth. We have handpicked exemplary narratives of individuals making quantum leaps, enabling reflective learning to strengthen your unique journey.

11.1. The Story of Rebecca: Unleashing Inner Potential

In our first case, we have Rebecca, a mid-level executive plagued by her fear of public speaking. She confronted this fear, opting for a quantum leap in her personal development path. Putting herself into various public speaking scenarios, from small group presentations to large auditorium addresses, she altered her mindset to perceive public speaking not as a threat, but as a challenge. Consequently, she liberated herself from the shackles of her fear, ushering in a new era of confidence and self-assurance, a quantum leap from her previous state.

11.2. The Transformation of Peter: Turning Failure into a Stepping Stone

Peter's narrative provides a unique perspective on failure. As an aspiring entrepreneur who encountered numerous setbacks, Peter was on the verge of giving up on his dream. However, he changed his approach, redefining the way he perceived failure. Perceiving his past failures as lessons, Peter made a quantum leap, pivoting his business concept, reworking his operational model based on the learning derived from his previous failures. His entrepreneurial venture is now genuinely successful.

11.3. Jane's Journey: Building Resilience and Bouncing Back

Jane, a successful corporate lawyer, faced an unexpected career setback when she was passed over for a much-anticipated promotion. Initially filled with despair, she decided to employ a quantum leap in her response strategy. Asserting a resilient mindset, she immersed herself in maximizing her skills and improving her areas of weakness. This renewed mindset escalated her professional development at an accelerated pace. In the following year, she leapt to a senior position in another prestigious law firm.

11.4. Matthew's Metamorphosis: The Quantum Leap in Embracing Change

Matthew's story embodies the essence of a quantum leap. An artist by profession, Matthew found his work abruptly disrupted by technological advances within his industry. Instead of resisting this change, he marshaled energy to understand and embrace digital art tools. Employing a radical shift in perspective and skills, he progressed from traditional painting techniques to digital artistry. This quantum leap in adaptability allowed him to revolutionize his art, earning him international recognition.

11.5. Natalie's Narrative: The Power of Effective Goal Setting

Our final example, Natalie, illustrates the power of effective goal setting as a manifestation of quantum leaps. Finding herself in a cycle of procrastination and inefficiency, Natalie redefined her personal development strategy. She applied a quantum approach to goal setting, using tools such as visualization, affirmations, and chunking. Consequently, she transformed her workplace productivity and achieved a level of efficiency she had previously deemed unattainable.

The stories highlighted in this chapter intend to inspire readers, driving home the point that quantum leaps aren't merely theoretical constructs. Quantum leaps in personal development are practical, applicable, and can foster meaningful transformation when appropriately harnessed. While each person's journey is unique, these case studies provide a roadmap, offering glimpses of the powerful growth that can be achieved by implementing quantum leap strategies. The aim is to empower you to take that exceptional leap, leading you on a transformative journey of self-discovery and unimaginable growth.

www.ingramcontent.com/pod-product-compliance
Lightning Source LLC
Chambersburg PA
CBHW070953220526
45471CB00007B/3013